CW01521277

LOVE WITHIN THE WORLD

Edited by

Sarah Marshall

First published in Great Britain in 2003 by
POETRY NOW
Remus House,
Coltsfoot Drive,
Peterborough, PE2 9JX
Telephone (01733) 898101
Fax (01733) 313524

HB ISBN 1 84460 932 4
SB ISBN 1 84460 933 2

FOREWORD

Although we are a nation of poets we are accused of not reading poetry, or buying poetry books. After many years of listening to the incessant gripes of poetry publishers, I can only assume that the books they publish, in general, are books that most people do not want to read.

Poetry should not be obscure, introverted, and as cryptic as a crossword puzzle: it is the poet's duty to reach out and embrace the world.

The world owes the poet nothing and we should not be expected to dig and delve into a rambling discourse searching for some inner meaning.

The reason we write poetry (and almost all of us do) is because we want to communicate: an ideal; an idea; or a specific feeling. Poetry is as essential in communication, as a letter; a radio; a telephone, and the main criterion for selecting the poems in this anthology is very simple: they communicate.

CONTENTS

TO WHAT SHALL I COMPARE YOU

Shall I compare you to a summer's day?
No, I'll compare you with spring's awakening!
Of snowdrops glistening in morning frost,
Frail and beautiful but unprotected,
Of birds singing after rain,
With ever joyful words to say,
Of violets standing sentinel o'er paths,
Dainty and fragile but ever watchful,
Of lambs frolicking in the fields,
Young and unsure and ever playful,
Of bluebells massing in the woods,
Proud and gregarious but often lonely,
Of blossom sprouting on the trees,
Colourful and pretty to behold.

Joe Loxton

THE INGREDIENTS FOR LOVE

I liked her and she liked me, could it be a sign it was meant to be?
When she smiled I smiled too, when she laughed my heart did too.
When she speaks I listened with ease, as she moves closer I go
weak at the knees.

Something's are meant to be, they say what should will find a way
But do two people ever fall for each other in the same way?

How are we meant to know if it's right?
How are we meant to distinguish what's wrong and what's right?
In the game of love it always seems to be one sided
But do two hearts ever collide and become united?

What is it we need to make love work,
What is needed to make a lover on earth?

Do you need friendship and trust
Or do you follow your instincts and go for desire and lust?
Do you go for someone who's single or maybe a friend
Or someone who's forbidden and only there in dreams?

The one you share interests with and could be happy with all day
Or the one who represents desire, passion and play come
whatever time of day?

The one that's pretty or the one who's divine
The one who'd bring safety, or the one who'd break
your heart in just a short time?

The answer should be clear and simple I know
But which one would *really* make you happy though?

Your heart leans to one and your head to the other,
But which one will become your lover?

Do you go for safety and trust, friendship and
companionship are surely a must
Or do you follow your heart and stick with danger
But expect inevitable pain from someone who's merely a stranger?

What are the ingredients we need for love, what is it we need for life?
Do we listen to the angel in our head
Or the devil with passion, mystery and excitement instead?

Do we follow our head or heart . . .

Lynsey Tocker

THE FOURTEENTH

When I was four, Valentine's meant so much more,
Roses are red, violets are blue,
Red tissue paper and paper doilies too.

Last year, finding a lunchtime free in our whirlwind week,
Chillies are red, I'll have vindaloo,
A romantic curry - certainly new!

The year before, glorious sunshine was the score,
The soup is red, Broadside a good brew,
Sat outside the Queen's Head, in February, it's true!

Quieter now, eyes across a restaurant table,
A bottle of red, mixed Metze for two,
Confident in my love for you.

Paula Holt

WOMAN IN LOVE

Bottled paradise, is that what you want
Slip him a Mickey and hope he responds
If only things were quite that pat
You're a woman in love,
You can't see beyond that.

You know you're being given the run-around chat
But still you think, he's the perfect catch
You'd never consider, calling his bluff
You're a woman in love,
That's more than enough.

It hurts so much, you can hardly sleep
Just to hear him say, 'I'm yours to keep,'
He doesn't even call, to ask how you are
You're a woman in love
And you're wearing the scar.

After all he's married, there's that to consider
With a wife and a mistress, he's on to a winner
No need for commitment, when his options are flying,
You're a woman in love,
But who's the one crying.

Tiny tears, that fall like Niagara
Is he worth it, your conscience nags yer,
Emotional outbursts, of the gymslip club
But you're not a schoolgirl,
You're a woman in love.

Michael Gardner

LOVE

Love means nothing
You think it's eternal
Show me two people truly in love
Everyone likes to say it
But when the moment comes
They'd sooner go and break it
That's all that love is
Only lies and deceit
Malicious lust, passions flame
It's not a game to be played
I'm not a girl to be used
Show me love and I'll show you
Twice as many hearts
Coldly broken in two.

Leanne Hanrahan

TO LOVE HER

To love her, I must know her
And hold her close, yet closer still.
So close, I breathe her deep inside
And taste her when we kiss.
Her every part against my skin,
Her warmth, I want to let flood in
And take my soul and then begin,
To feel sweet love I've missed.

Could she love me? Would she take me?
To her care, I give my soul.
Oh, I have missed the times I kissed her,
Died some when we've been apart.
So hold me close and I'll hold you,
Please tell me now what I must do,
But say you will be mine so true,
For no one else will have my heart.

S Joyce

PROMISE

I have poetry inside me.
Enough to sing the world of your enchanting eyes,
And as we weave our fairytale, through scene on laughing scene,
I'll pen such verse as none compare, rejoicing of our lives.

Andrew Hirst

THAT'S WHAT YOU ARE!

You consume and enthral me
The thing's you say and do enchant me
My love for you I can't explain
But all is black when I think I'm not to see you again
With every beat of my heart
I yearn for you
You are dearer to me than any one . . .
And that's the truth
Sweet and incomparable
That's what you are!

Lynn Thompson

ONE

One you
One me
One us
One boy
One girl
One family
No addings on
No takings away
No multiple complications
We're one.

Clare Todd

ONE DAY I ASKED MY BELOVED

One day I asked my beloved
How much do you love me?
My beloved replied:
My love is not contained in words
But fills the oceans of this world and the next
It cannot remain in me alone
For it is boundless energy that echoes throughout the universe
Not even a single heartbeat, a drop of the purest water or
The luminous glow of the moon can compare to the
                                    infinite power of love
It shines lighter than the brightest star
Is greater than the highest mountain
And will remain a burning flame throughout eternity
Close your eyes, quieten your mind, open your heart
                                    and all will be realised.

Varsha Maisuria

LOSING YOU...

I'm falling in love with you
And I can't stop myself
I know why now, you have so many men
Oh, God, I look to the heavens
To brake myself, and I see only stars

I'm falling in love with you
And I can't stop myself
And yet I must
For without brakes I will lose you
Worse, disgust you -
I hear your voice in my head and without brakes
You will destroy me

Are you? No, I'm not, I couldn't be
And yet I'm falling
Ever closer to disaster
I'm falling and I hate myself
And I have no hope that you will stop me

I'm falling, ever closer to the egress
And yet I love you, falling constantly
Only to be reminded to the solid, braking stop
Which will await me
Losing you in totality, your voice empty in my head
Falling, to splatter across, the end of your stay
Devoid and without you, the void closing in upon my soul again -
Knowing you are gone.

Jennifer Cook

WITH LOVE - FOR ALWAYS

Together for always
Those were the words
You are the one girl for me
That's what you told me
The day that we met
That's how it's going to be
The years have gone by
We weathered the storms
Together we stood side by side
Through good times and bad times
Times for gay laughter
You held me close when I cried
Till death do us part
Was the vow that we made
And now I am left all alone
Trying to cope with each lonely day
No pleasure in life now you're gone
But I shall never forget you
Though now we are so far apart
Still we're together for always
Always - here in my heart.

Lydia Barnett

EVER IN THE HEART

Her eyes were bright,
her cheeks were wet,
as she listened to the waves
gently lapping on the shore.
For she knew that he was gone for evermore.

Her heart ached to see him again.
Her heart was broken
and she knew she would never be whole
without the loved one
who disappeared so long ago last year.

How could she go on all alone?
How could she ever feel alive again?
Her nearest and dearest,
her soul mate and friend, had been taken from her.
Never to return.

Eve McGrath

LONELY FOOTSTEPS

Lonely footsteps in the clouds,
Shedding teardrops to hit the ground.
Lonely footsteps in the grass,
A moment's thought, all things must pass.
Lonely footsteps on the earth,
A gust of wind, footsteps prints disappear,
Blown away into the air,
Lonely footsteps on the beach,
Taken as the tide turns into the cruel sea.
Lonely footsteps in the mind,
Worried over troubled times,
Lonely footsteps at the end of a life,
As the final curtain draws shut,
Lonely footsteps return unto dust.

Phil Clayton

TAJ MAHAL (A SHRINE TO LOVE)

If I'd been the Shah Jahan,
And you'd been Mumtaz i Mahal,
I'd have planned out a fabulous palace,
And built you a Taj Mahal,
I don't care if it took me forever,
And cost me a fortune as well,
It just wouldn't matter a jot to me,
If it made you smile, all would be well:
My love for you is eternal,
Just like Shah Jahan's for Mumtaz,
I'd build you a shrine in white marble,
Looking like it had been washed in Daz,
If you find my devotion is lacking,
Just tell me and you can be sure,
It'll all be put right in a moment,
You couldn't be loved any more!

Mick Nash

ISOLATION

Outside,
The howl of a dog,
The distant toiling of a train,
Drop almost unnoticed
Into the vast silence of the moon-silvered night.
Here,
As we sit before the fire, my love,
Time holds its breath.
The leaping pattern of the flames,
The hissing of damp logs,
The flung sparks glowing for a moment
On the soot-laden fire-back-
These only serve to deepen
The profound stillness which enfolds us.
Soon enough, my dear one,
The thronging world will force its way
Into our isolation;
But, for this moment,
We will drink deep of each other,
And the stillness,
And the leaping fire-glow.

Peter English

FOR YOUR PROTECTION

Whatever life brings your way
Surrender
Surrender to the situation,
Find another way.
Look deep inside, the answer's always there, within.
Just be your love,
It is for your protection.

Life will only give, what life knows you can handle,
You have the inner strength.
In the busyness of your mind, stop, count to ten,
Breathe deeply, go still
Somewhere inside you have the strength,
Search for the connection, it will come.
Just be your love,
It is for your protection.

When you feel emotional,
The disturbance, something is not right,
The discomfort and the pain.
Emotion is to tell you something's wrong.
It is not the body, yet it is within.
Just be your love,
It is for your protection.

When you cannot find the words,
To help a friend,
To lend a hand,
Stop - listen - it is not for you to speak.
Just be your love,
It is for your protection.

When you feel moody, sulky, angry, frustrated,
That's when your little child within is hurting.
The task of running your life is just too great,
For the little child.
Stop - listen - to the voice within,
Just be your love,
It is for your protection.

Kathy Watchorn

THE IMPOSSIBLE ROMANCE

A couple meet for the very first time
They seem to gel and get on fine
Their thoughts towards each other benign
'Can I see you again?' - the usual line.

Now conversation flows and feelings soar
As two minds meet with genuine rapport
Two hearts blend, love flowing to the core
Each thinking that this is - forevermore.

To last forever, till death us do part
That we could have the mind and heart
To know it would last from the very start
In perfect harmony, like a tune from Mozart.

Michael J Pritchard

YOU BEING YOU

Every beginning proves
itself elusive
but you, being you,
makes it easy to start.
So the rest, now begun,
is conclusive especially
as you have captured my heart.

The sailor at your side
last night remembered
the sea again. Walking along
a seashore, searching and finding
a shell, I listened
hearing the sound
of your voice as never before.

(Reminded of your soft murmurings
in satiety after your shrill
cries of delight.)
Whilst it lasted our love was
a duality till divine decree
passed it into night.

For nothing is so conclusive
as death and now know,
at this ending, of its stealth
and your enduring strength.

Michael Alan Fenton

HIS FRIEND

Homeless,
No family,
No money,
All his possessions in a ragged rucksack.
His chair,
His bed,
The hard pavement.
He watched the hurrying feet,
Heard the roar of traffic,
Smelt the petrol fumes.
Remembered -
The harsh words,
The arguments,
The violence,
The rejection.
Life torn apart,
The loss of all he had held dear.
Despair,
Anguish,
And then -
He looked down,
Looked into those loving
Warm brown eyes.
Yes, he was loved,
Still loved,
And now his frozen heart
Could thaw and love again.
No longer lonely
He gathered her into his arms,
Felt her heart beat against his own,
Her warmth reaching into his cold body,
Knew he was richly blessed and loved
By his four-footed friend.

Roma Davies

JOURNEY TO LOVE

Lonely nights, waiting games,
Stolen glances, code names,
Forbidden love, bitter-sweet,
Married man, rotten cheat,
Aching heart, hurtful words,
Piercing eyes, love birds,
Mixed emotions, desperate times,
Complete devotion, pick-up lines,
Growing children, complications,
Going without, deprivation,
Bound as one, love or lust?
Together forever, so unjust,
Never mine, shared affection,
Hopeless case, heart protection,
Gossip mongers, quest for freedom,
Unbounded love, listen to reason,
One way ticket, so unfair,
No going back, never there,
Confidantes, special friends,
Secret lives, social trends,
Rendezvous, hideaways,
Meeting places, better days,
Lessons learned, warning signs,
Emotional pain, hearts entwined,
Alone together, kindred spirits,
Everlasting love, no limits.

K E Evans

MICHAELA

Michaela, Michaela,
You are my love's saviour
When my times arrives and no days remain
My feelings for you will remain the same

Although I feared the possibility of never reaching out
The love I hold inside, leaves me in no doubt
For the mere thought of proving my love to you
Mesmerises my soul, where insecurities once grew

Walking through shadows, trying to find the light
I see you stand alone in the middle of my night
I feel submerged in the purity that enraptures my soul
Someone planted the seeds for my aching heart to grow

And as we travel across very different lands
One day I know we'll both be holding hands
For the hands of fate we all walk upon
Shape the sky of many tender song

So walk on and keep on walking
For the journey never ends, it simply changes
And I will walk with you for a part of the way
So until we hold hands, goodbye until some day.

Paul Dawson

PARTING

Like sparkling wine outpoured
The silvery sheen of the sea,
In halcyon calm of sunlight days
My love and I seek sandy bays.
Time for kisses
At the parting of our ways
But darkling changes come,
Great breakers roll over the sea,
Roll higher with each succeeding wave,
We'll run and shelter in that cave,
It's not very discreet,
But very sweet,
And your kisses make me brave.
As thundery peaks roll forth
They echo over the sea,
Vivid lightning sweeps over the sky
Dazzling to the beholder's eyes;
We know at heart
It's time to part,
But wait until the storm rolls by.
Wait until the clouds roll by,
From our hearts, storm-tossed as the sea,
Agony frozen in every vein,
How can we ever love again?
Darling this is
Last of kisses,
As we part in mutual pain . . .

E Osmond

BETRAYAL

I remembered the lines of an old song
Lipstick on your collar told a tale on you
How true
The lipstick on your collar wasn't mine.

You smelled of Dior's Poison
A perfume I detest
The restaurant bill left carelessly on your bureau
Intimated a romantic dinner for two.

The phone conversations hastily ended
When I entered the room
The biggest give-away ignoring my best friend
When you saw her at a party.

Your excuses became transparent
Growing thinner by the day
Stripped down to a tissue of lies
That had covered your deceit.

I could have ranted and raved
But by now I no longer cared
I packed my broken heart in a suitcase
And left without a word.

Adrianne Jones

MY JULIET

My love is the reflection on a lake
My love is the face in every day dreams
My love is the colours of the rainbow
My love is that early morning mist.

And when I embrace her, my heart stands still
The sun shines through the clouds,
The land loses its early morning chill,
All my being, it comes to one.

Our love is more than the world around
Our love is more than all I trust
And though I stand my presence confined
I feel a destiny of love.

Les Allen

LOVE'S GONE

I never thought I'd lose you
I never thought you'd go
I never thought you'd hate me
Then turn to tell me so
The words you used to curse me
Have made the job well done
The words you used to hurt me
Have bade my love be gone
What seized your heart?
And tore your love from mine
What wrapped itself around you
And crept within your mind?

L J Doel

COMETS AND SHINING LIGHTS

In the vast expanses of space
A bright star formed and shone
It burnt more brightly than the sun
And it was destined to be our 'one'

It did light our world but briefly
And it put on such a show
That the darkness left behind
Did make one sad and low

As its light doth fade the memory
We can remember only the good
Its purpose being complete then
We wouldn't change it if we could

Before you knew it, it had gone
We looked one last time in awe
Do others see the same thing?
And do those others want it more?

What we had we will never forget
Its very warmth affected us all
From a being that's so complex
Why did it choose us to pay a call?

It started life in a cosmic place
Its beam falling on but a few
It shone its brightest when it was near
And for a moment it fell on you

But you can't and shouldn't hold on
As fast as it came the light had gone
It slipped like sand through our fingers
Leaving stardust memories and fun

In its speedy departure the skies were grey and bleak
I think its very passing had burnt us out
But it taught us both such a valuable lesson
It taught us what love was all about

A faint glow still illuminates, that cold and blackened sky
But we were so very lucky it came our way
And like all comets and shining lights
It will shine again some day.

Michael Bellerby

YOU WERE WISER

Your eyes took in everything
You were wiser
Everyone was so stupid
You knew so much
They were so thick
They were older
But you were wiser
Your eyes shone
With that sparkle
Of knowing
You took it all in
Your eyes beamed
With love
Undimmed by hate
You knew.

Greig Linton

VACATION'S LOVES

Their wistful hearts so sadly lie
In drifts of autumn's leaves
Where summer's loves, unnourished, waste away.

And feelings yearn
Though once, they blazed in warmth and light.
But ardour, now in shadows, pines away.

There, with sun-kissed hands, they touched;
Between them now stretch sterile miles,
And drab routines will isolate and quench desire.

Attraction ever lays its seasonal snares
In leisured walks and sunlit beach
Where blinding light no tempering doubts allow.

Other suns and other times
Will surely snare the vulnerable.
What promised bridges *will* they built to couple distant love?

Much better then in drifts of leaves
Those yearning hearts should rest.
For truly, summer's light and warmth deceives.

Ron Hails

SEPIA LOVE

At first sight it was
instant love.
An explosion of emotion.
A physical agony
of immense intensity.

He had to possess her.
Those eyes eager and searching
consumed his waking.
That smile pervaded his dreams.

Final self criticism
confirmed the pathetism.
A professor in love with a century old
sepia car boot sale beauty.

Michael N McKimm

DREAMS

Here in the early hours, I think of you,
Warm and peaceful in sleep,
Knowing I will never be with you,
Yet my dreams I keep.

Now as day approaches, I think of you,
Waking from the deep,
Knowing I will never be with you,
Yet my dreams I keep.

Sounds of the day threaten, and I think of you
As silently I weep,
Knowing I will never be with you,
Yet my dreams I keep.

Erica Sillett

VOLCANIC LOVE

A single star shines bright
I have reached the summit
Evening lingers neath a dark blue mantle
I hear the goat bell tinkle
Echoing down the valley green
My heart is wide awake
Close to my companion
Journeying in a dream.

The nostalgic odours
Of meadow sweet and purple clover
Fills the drowsy air
Stay sweet image stay awhile
Cling to this flimsy fantasy
A slender golden thread
A gleaming strand
A hand held posy of sweet scented buds
Whose fragrance drifts
To solitary hills.

Let the mountain erupt
Let the lava flow
I know, I know so well
Our volcanic love
Forbidden upon earth
Is throbbing beating still
Deep in the heart of the mountain
Like two white swans we swim
In heaven's pool
And bathe forever
In the sacred fountain of love.

Beth Izatt Anderson

STAR-CROSSED LOVE

It's all in the planets
When you were first born
Fate decides who crosses
Your path and enters your life

Painful lessons sometimes learnt
Hearts broken on either side
Tears shed in the darkness
Of the night.

Hopeless situations that
Cannot be resolved
Desperation at every twist
And turn

A parting of the ways
Nothing stays the same
Heartfelt happiness will
One day we hope return.

Candida Lovell-Smith

ETERNAL SUNSET

If I had time to paint
the short story of us,
utopia would beckon
through haunted gates.

For us it was always sunset,
for I am blinded by its beauty,
unable to move;
nocturnal;
eternal.

You weren't winter sun
But bright and alive;
Scorching black devil trees.
Gnarled.
Looming.

Will they seal our final requiem?
Damned to a cold winter dawn.

Daniel Watson

IN MY DREAM

You know in my dream I wanted to kiss you
I could see your pretty face with a wicked smile -
Hair and clouds rolled into one.

As you passed through the fence
Trying desperately to elude me
Like a magnet I followed.

So overwhelmed wanting to kiss you
But still you ran - my heart pounding.

Terry Lane

BLEAK DAYS

My heart shattered into a thousand pieces
You left suddenly without goodbye
Shallow emptiness filled me with despair
Surrounded by cold ice like a winter's day
The hours drag by never-ending
Bleakly walking the path ahead
Tears flowing from my eyes
Everlasting adoration of your memory
Stay close to me.

Olive M Poole

MEMORY

Memories colour even when distant
and nothing to do with the present.
Clamp on the lid of things
that make up the past
close eyes to everything
that was
There must be a known moment
in long goodbyes
when stretched emotions snap
and all that is left
is spent.

F A C

TIME

The days pass quickly, yet slowly for me;
for I fell into the sleep.
Through hazy eyes I see the moon shine, and the sun.
The flowers smile and close again,
as the sand grains fall and the wax burns away.

I hear nothing but my thoughts, feel nothing but the sand,
but how I wish I was with you.

Be on your guard my friend, for it watches all you do.
It listens to your heart; hiding, always waiting.
Waiting for the moment you close your eyes.
Waiting to pounce; to drag you into those shadows past.

Do not sleep, my love:
Don't drift into a memory - like an open trap,
but as the bells chime, reach for the day.

Don't think of me when the rays strike the dial.
Forget my voice as the hourglass loses.
But I'll remember you forever.

Beyond this rain of sand, I watch and pray,
and forget I've lost your smile.

Johanna Williamson

YOUNG LOVE

How she flirted with her teenage sweetheart,
Teased him with her golden curls,
Made promises so lightly, which he kept in his heart
Four long summer months they held each other,
Kissed and planned. He gazed into her open eyes,
Held her tiny hand. They would never part.

With the chill of autumn he found her love less true.
He would not let himself believe
This goodness, his own beloved,
Could fail, could fall, could fabricate.
Her lovely face, her body and her laugh
Could turn from him, be filled with other thoughts.

His fierce love unwavered, blind, intense,
He trusted his beloved still.
He would hear no word of difference.
His devotion was still blind.
All warning, advice, persuasion,
All suggestion, counsel brushed aside.

As she gradually grew away from him,
Laughed and played with other men,
He still stayed true and loyal
Fondly thinking things would change
Would alter with each day or week.
Perhaps this phase a pause, an interim.

One day he saw her with another man.
Oblivious of his gaze, she laughed
As she had laughed when he had held her.
Then turned a taunting back, her eyes
Ablaze with passion, her tiny hand held fast.
They hurried furtively, ran

Out of sight . . . his head span, heart a whirl.
He stood unmoving; then the tears began.
Sobbing he wandered towards his flat . . .
Lay on the bed where they had loved . . .
He tried to face reality, sat in the gloom;
Hurt, lost, betrayed, without his girl . . .

Jane England

MEDIEVAL KNIGHT

I am your medieval knight
I sit at the table by the door
I watch you, I watch you swaying on the dance floor
I sit in golden armour ready to defend your honour
I am ready for your call
You see me in working clothes, if you see me at all
I see you in the half-light leaving as you always do
Laughing with your friends
I sit a while longer until my strength returns
Then mount my white charger and ride into the gloom
I'll live in the ugly world until next Saturday night
Then I will put on my golden armour and ride to your side
Ready to defend your honour, ready for your call, make you my bride
But you'll leave without seeing laughing as you go
I am your medieval knight
Wearing city clothes.

Robert Denis Spencer

SILENT WORLD

A world of total silence
No wind
No cars
No voices
Nothing
Not even a whisper
Now imagine, if you can
The world of the deaf.

Kevin Huntley

ADORATION

I have been told secretly that you really do love me
    Why me? Of all people did you choose me as you agree
Plaguing me with gifts and your many extra pleasantries
    I am overwhelmed as you simply and truly adore
Pleading please, please, I want some breathing space
    You suffocate me with your amours still I implore
Control yourself and do behave you might send me in a rage
    Quieten down as I explain I cannot return love all is in vain
Taken back and astonished I see tears in those dear blue eyes
    You imagined I had promised to become your loving bride
This courtship is disastrous you are so eager to propose
    I do not appreciate your generosity even when you proffer a
                            single rose
Looking sad and awkward I feel so sorry in a motherly sort of way
    You look like a little boy lost one who has permanently gone astray
Dry your eyes you will find another who will be more fitting to suit
    I am ready a wife and mother you are overwhelmed I have
                            told the truth.

R D Hiscoke

DILEMMA

I cannot bring myself to put it all in words.
We only have your friends. Mine have been discouraged.
And when your friends ring up, and you're not there,
I have to admit I don't know where you are,
Nor yet with whom.
And, when I meet them, they have that shifty look,
That says they know more about us than they should.
Many other things disrupt our life.

If I did speak out about the way we live,
I don't think I would sound convincing,
Perhaps not to myself, and certainly not to you.
Your glorious eyes would redden, mist and brim.
A tear would trickle down your troubled cheek,
And I'd be lost - because I love you still.
I could not bear the awful silence,
That suffocating silence, which would last for several
Days and nights. I am torn apart.

I cannot live, like this, with you,
Nor can I live without you.

Robert T Collins

MY RING

I had a diamond ring in my finger
Somehow the precious gem fell off the ring

I searched for it in growing anger
While my heart in despair was sinking

But wisdom told me to look after
The dim metal left in my finger.

No bell would ring for such a dull thing,
No one can fool me and say a different thing

Until one evening.

When my eyes caught something sparkling
Disbelief kept me from going closer or asking

It was my gem, the one that used to be only mine
I found it on a new finger with all its glory and shine

Sorrow seized my heart and left me trembling
I couldn't remember my words, I was mumbling

A decade went by I knew no pleasure
My jewel became someone else's treasure

My soul was uprooted I felt it true,
And my senses all scattered I became blue

I lost feelings of joy and pain altogether
The lofty dream, which kept me alive, is now over

I left my glass on the table half full
To no destination I look my empty soul.

Adouda Adjiri

TO MY LOVE ON VALENTINE'S DAY

You are my Valentine, dear love,
My heart to you I give
With all my love
In sun and rain.
Down the long reaches
Of the steeps of time
When winter's white
Changes to summer's gold
And back again.
My love is steadfast
And forever grows
And blossoms sweet
As any red, red rose.

Margaret B Baguley

THE SPARE ROOM
(To the memory of Charlotte Wilson)

Without - no more than a home's dumping ground
for junk like board games and broken gadgets.

The wealth of spareness, though, is deceptive.
Those who had loved would rather possess it.

Carefully gathered, in the cupboard lie
hand-written letters - fragments of desire.

Like children, with fireballs, two lovers played.
Sure it was the death-dream-distance drew them.

And scheming still for happiness, we trust,
as likely, without, the dust will come too,
it is these that would possess the room now.

Ben Pollitt

OUR WALK IN LAUGHTON FOREST

Afternoon,
The rain falls between the bluebells,
We wait under a beech
And the whole wood smells green.

I thumb moss from the tree's bark
And stud your smile and when it does not
Also your eyes when they do and when they do not -
And know you don't love me,
Not like that.
The sun feels dark here.

Ivy chats sinisterly overhead
The sun has stopped shining.
The ferns and hogweed wrapping our feet.
Cowslips shrink away
Into the hedge and far horizon.

Two peasants pounce past
Slapping the startled air
And spanking the flat grass,
You watch,
And I kiss your wet mouth.

Doreen Sylvester

FORBIDDEN LOVE

How could I not remember you?
Though long ago when we were young.
Forbidden love it was yet true
a love song that remains unsung.
The longing that I still recall;
so obvious then for all to see.
The yearning just to give our all
yet no future could there be.

Fulfilment was a need I sought
whenever I was close to you.
My body and my mind were fraught,
with passion I could not subdue.

Those precious hours that we had shared
for just awhile to ease the pain.
Postponing thoughts of future years,
when we would be alone again.
Our parting did not change my heart
so wearisome has time passed by,
without your arms to hold me close:
but I will love you till I die.

Molly Phasey

MY VALENTINE

My husband, my valentine,
Thinks a lot of me,
When we met he courted me with chocolates
Which we shared in the cinema,
He put his arm around me,
I thought my heart would *stop!*
And later, we enjoyed fish and chips
He smelt of soap and aftershave
I can remember today,
We married, had four children,
Which have grown up and moved away,
As they grew, we shared laughter and tears,
I remember, when it rained
He took his jacket off for me to wear
And he got *wet,*
Now years later as we grow older,
We say have you got your mack dear,
He holds my hand to steady me,
So that I won't fall.
Such silent love between us
No chocolates now! But flowers
Which *won't* make me fat.
He will always be my Valentine
Oh! Where did I put my hat?

Joan M Waller

GOODBYE

How dare you keep those feelings,
so aware that they're forbidden.
Hand me a scalpel,
I'll surgery them - out of you
scrape away the excess
and make - it - into - guilt.
But you're etched on my aorta,
embedded in my grey matter,
sewn into my skin.
I chiselled into your name
that's tattooed upon my brain.
Cramped are my lips
numb to the tips
words of water stream -
from my eyes that gleam
at the last moment
a - fore - goodbye,
dead is love - goodbye.

Helen McGachy

GRETA

Greta, be still;
Your race were foes of mine
And laid my father low
With one shell fired from an unseeing gun.
No call to join in Hell
The father whom you once adored.

Greta, be still
Beneath that stone among these northern graves
Where once they laid you fifty years ago
And I bid you goodbye,
And now I, tired with years
Look down on you and feel the ache again.

Greta, be still.
Your laughter's with us yet
As in our student days.
Tall, slender, fair, with kindling eyes,
Soft lips which only spoke of happy things
But mine alone to kiss.

Cherished by all
You were my special prize
To walk among these northern towers and hills,
Make love in summer fields, know only joy,
Free of our fathers' sins.
Lie still; I'll not forget.

Your father's sins! He burned a thousand Jews.
You learned of this - it blew your soul away,
Turned your high noon into the blackest night,
Led you to break your body from the bridge.
Since then I've learned to lock my heart away.
Be still, my Greta, where you still are loved.

Philip Worth

THE STORY OF US

It's the story of us,
of two hearts beating fast,
between the sheets and the stars.

It's the story of us,
of what has been and what's to come
between the present and the past.

It's the story of us,
random fighting and making-up
between the tears and the laughs.

It's the story of us,
a game of truth and dare
of the, 'I wish you were there'.

It's the story of us,
an eternal fairy tale
between two rings and a veil.

It's the story of us,
a white dress
and a hundred guests.

It's the story of us
and I know that it will last.

Giovanni Nacci

YOUR EYES

Your eyes were my first delight,
Deep piercing blue.
I instantly fell in love with you.

Your dance was divine,
We merged together
With the rhythm of love.
Our souls combined and
We were forever entwined,
In our hearts and in our minds.

That was when we first met.
You were 17 and had that
Marvellous flush of youth.
I will never forget, that first
Time we met.

It seems but a moment in time,
But it's been 23 years since.
Where did our time go?
That's what I want to know.

We always wish we had made
Better use of our time together.
But there's no going back to change
The things you thought, you lacked.
All we can do, is learn from the past.

Think of your triumphs.
Think of all the happy time,
When love was the only thing that mattered,
Before your dreams were blasted,
Shattered and scattered.

Roberta West

THE TYPE OF VALENTINE, AND FUTURE HUSBAND I WOULD HAVE LIKED

My valentine would have been a six-footer,
Sturdy, with shrewd grey eyes.
Capable of great strength, but a gentle giant besides.
He would have taken great care of me,
But would have expected me to be independent, too,
We should have shared many a hobby
And had some similar points of view.

Marjorie Cowan

To A Woman

This is to a woman called Carol
Who will never be mine
This is to a woman who's beauty
Will outlast *even time.*

I will never hold you
In my arms
I will never feel
Your warm tender love
Or soft sweet charms
I will never look into
Your angel blue eyes
Or kiss your soft and sweet
Ruby red lips.

For you are an angel
From heaven above
And angels never come down
To Earth below
And if they ever do
It's only at *night*
And Christmas time.

Donald John Tye

UNTITLED

Crashing down,
No moving,
No stopping,
Just waterfalls surrounding my lips
So blind
Can't see through the rain
Rivers around my eyes,
Puddle surround my feet.
I'm drowning in pain.

The pain inside crushes my mind,
Every memory is shadowed
Every thought is overtaken by hate,
I will never love again,
I will never again understand.
I fall asleep and dream,
Wishing I could believe in love again,
I wish I could believe that love goes on.

A world I've never seen flows through my heart,
My mind visits another dimension
Dreams pass over to reality and my imagination grows stronger.
Never leaving my heart, always in my mind.
A part of my soul.

Donna Moulding

VALENTINE'S EVE

On a velvet seat
She sat alone.
Red paper hearts
And flowers
Did nothing
To soften the thorns
That pricked her heart.
The music flowed
The lamplight gleamed
And others danced.
Cupid's arrows were tipped
With gall.
The roses, the kisses
Were not for her
But she wanted them
With all her heart.

Fran Barker

VALENTINE 2002

I think about you all of the time,
You're forever on my mind,
No matter how hard I try,
Nothing can stop me dreaming of you,
Only of you,
Wishing you would feel the same about me too.

My heart flutters at the sound of your voice,
I hang onto your every word like it's the last,
It doesn't take a lot to get me through the day,
Just some evidence so I know that you're okay.

I dream about you every night,
Or just lay awake thinking,
Wishing you were here with me,
To hold me close, to keep me warm and happy.

In reality it doesn't seem very likely,
But in my dreams it sometimes seems,
That being with you, someday far away,
Isn't impossible at all.

Heidi Dungate

WE KNOW THE FEELING

The feeling of being loved,
And loved in return,
It is a beautiful thought,
A beautiful feeling,
That brings you to tears.

Nothing is so ultimate,
Than the feeling
Of deep integrity,
Of deeper dignity,
Of intense pride.

It is a perfect feeling
A wonderful way to live,
A feeling of wanting,
A feeling of need
It is so natural.

You have a feeling,
Of loving the one,
That you crave for,
Once it was quiet,
But now, you burst open,
Your deeper feelings.

Of wanting the essential,
Because there is nothing so precious,
Than the one who gives you the feeling,
Of having a brain,
Of feeling young and dignified again.

Zaynab Armstrong-Jones

SAINT VALENTINE DAY

Darling, how beautiful the world
Is today sitted with you on
That bay watching photogenic waterfalls
Dolphins and porpoises leaping in cheerfulness
Balloons in full flight
Across a clear blue sky
Fireworks of rose flowers exploding
Sky high like a Roman candle
The snow in free fall

Darling, how beautiful you are
In my arms on this
Saint Valentine Day
Hair pony-tailed
Your outfit a rose garden
Wearing a full moon smile
Nightingales hopping from one
Rose bush to another
Singing sweet love songs
Your eyes big, round and glazing
Your full lips against mine
Taste sweeter than wine
My gift to you a bouquet of roses
Oh, love's passion doses
Sinking on the bottomless
Pond of love this day
Love reduces us to mere kids
We forget our differences
And melt with this lovely day.

Cuthbert Makwetura

VALENTINE'S DAY FOR ONE LEFT

Such happy memories though tears flow with them
Your hand in mine, when love made a child of me
Love romantic but sincere as were your lovely eyes
Reflecting mine with honest commitment to each other
Heralding our promised path of devoted loyalty
Eyes that could laugh with me - or at me - as they pleased
How could such love let us be cross for long?
All those exchanged smiles - when Heaven sang
And when instantly recognising the many songs we loved
At one and the same moment - such bliss sublime
Love meant we valued both our strengths and weaknesses
Caring intimately for both like precious jewels
Safely seeing us through those times of resentment,
Of anger, sadness and blue moods that soon passed
Under love's spell - one by one they fell away
Always, always, each other's face so treasured
Forever reminding us when first we fell for one another
Love brought delight in surprises, flowers and welcome gifts
Frank motivations of truth - once discovered - ever saved.
Love so ached for good lights to end any tunnel
Reliably capitulated with assured hope, not fear.
It's simple - the two of us together - as God designed.

I'm left bereaved now, of course, and some years on
But that river of love could never stop flowing
So many brothers and sisters left, as I am - know its truth
Ever valuing wonderful memories of such caring ways
Living each day like me, blessed by love in Heaven.
Then join with me, this happy Valentine's Day,
Knowing for sure - our day of forever -
    Has yet to come.

Don Harris

LOVE POETRY

Oh Valentine, my Valentine,
Today my love I sent to you
In years past and those to come
It was and is steadfast and true.

Your every wish and every thought
Is priceless in my eyes,
The sunshine of your smile
Lights up the darkest skies.

Where're you go, what're you do
I'll be always by your side;
My love will last forever
'Til the flames of Vesuvius abide.

Robert H Quin

BE MY VALENTINE

My one and only,
True love,
Has gone far away.
Just as he left,
He handed me a card,
Which read:
This little card
Is from Jess,
Wishing you all the best,
Hope you get it just in time,
So I can be your
Darling Valentine.

E Bevans

A HAPPY TIME, MY VALENTINE

Will you be my valentine?
As I hope to make you, my lovely, mine
Your eyes so blue, remind me to be true
Of the blue sky above and are one of the
Reasons why I love, dear heart, but you
Your lips do hold a soft repose
Your laugh does gladden my heart
And like a rose, your sweet perfume upon
My senses grows, and keeps my thoughts
Tender aye, towards you
Will you be my Valentine? Won't you let me
Make you mine?
Take my heart, my love at this now time
May it be a joy, to ever remember.

Margaret Lightbody

THE HEART

The heart is a locked chest.
Love is its treasure.
Everyone has a key.
Who's heart will it open?
Nobody knows.
Meanwhile all the love grows,
Like a flower.
Everyone forgets its hidden power.
When a key finds its heart,
It gives the owner quite a start.
The love inside it, I hope will last forever,
Keeping two people together.
The heart.

Nicole Woollard

VALENTINE'S DAY

I dreamed of you last night.
Even though I remembered on waking
that you are the other side of the world,
I still felt a closeness and joy,
because in my dream you came to me,
planted a special kiss on my cheek
and said, 'I love you, and that is *for ever.*'
That was my only consolation,
knowing that you are still thinking of me
with that old comforting way of yours.
All those thousands of miles between us
shrank to nothing.
My morning was lifted to unreal heights,
as memories were rekindled of happier days
together in the garden or by the fireside.
We planted for the future, you and me,
with images of next year's daffodils,
and Easter Evensong a glorious hour,
to give us hope and happiness and love
enough for both, with plenty more to give away.
While we are apart, my Valentine,
I mark the days off on the calendar,
and practise all those lovely words to say
to you, when you return for real.

J G Mellis

DEPARTING KISS

Death took the man from me,
And stole the life
I loved dearly.
It crushed all my dreams
Like a thief in the night
It stole a priceless treasure,
And like a phantom it crept
Through the dark
And preyed on a weak victim.
Death cast its shadow
Over me,
A black cloud
That weighs heavily upon
My shoulders.
Death is a force
I cannot defeat,
It left the ghost
Of the man I love.
Death took the man
From me,
And left its cold
Trademark of an
Absent lover.
It touched me
In its passing
And spoke to me in a
Cold breath;
And my man, before he
Fell asleep, kissed
Me one last time.

C A Keohane

LOVE, BEAUTIFUL LOVE

There comes a time when love reaches a certain stage,
and your love for each other has come of age.
The expressions of love take many forms,
some by action, spoken words and charms.
It is special to make a public declaration,
tell the world of your love and true intention.
It's wonderful when a man and a woman get committed,
you know their love is true and unlimited.
It's almost Heaven when a man and a woman are truly in love,
what can compare to love, beautiful love.

When you are in love, it makes you feel glad,
fall out of love and it makes you feel sad.
The feeling of love is a wonderful feeling,
without love the feeling is nothing.
Love cannot always be expressed in words,
so action speak for some love birds.
Love is something you can't see but you can feel,
love is a powerful force that is so real.
You don't ask, you know when you I love,
what can compare to love, beautiful love.

Two hearts of gold are a priceless treasure,
like magnet and steel they hold on to each other.
Where there is true love there is happiness,
give one hundred percent of love no less.
It takes two halves of love to make one heart,
love keeps you together, hate keeps you apart.
To give your heart and soul is a gift of love,
what can compare to love, beautiful love.

Barrington Delevante

My One Redeeming Grace

God knows I love you for I often tell Him so
And I suppose He also knows how much.
But it is still a wonderment to me
That you can fill so many needs of love, such
As to be the son we've never had; the brother;
The never boring companion and the lover -
Confident, playmate, friend, master and man
Always to my life's end. A feeling so strong it can
Transcend age, time, distance, space and ever be
My one redeeming grace - my love for thee.

Isabel Samwells

NOT QUITE NORMAL

When I look into your beautiful eyes,
And you're looking into mine,
Everything feels not quite normal,
I'm strong but weak at the same time,

I feel excited but yet terrified,
Truth is I don't know how I feel,
But I know just where I want to be,
Around you I'm me, it's real,

It's as though I've reached the unreachable,
And I wasn't quite ready yet,
But no matter how it makes me feel,
I'm so glad that you I met,

One day I'll figure these feelings out,
But until I reach that day,
I'll be in love with you always,
And that's where I want to stay.

Mitch Cokien

SOMEONE

Someone to love, to care and to share,
The fun and the laughter and always be there.
Someone to sense when you're feeling down,
Someone whose smile can erase every frown.
Someone who knows all your fears and your ways,
Someone who brightens the darkest of days.
Someone to lean on when things go all wrong,
But in turn to be there when his strength's not so strong.
Someone we knew when we were both young,
So that time never changed us
Nor the love song we sung.

Shirley Wasylyk

ANDREA AND CARL'S WEDDING CELEBRATIONS

Let's rush to the pub
In horse and carriage,
Andrea and Carl are getting married,
Ale, wine, spirits and food for all,
To count all the guests,
Too close to call.

Andrea and Carl are looking for a home,
But the pub is their home,
Where as barmaid and chef
They can strike a treble and tenor cleft.

I love them both,
They are my friends.
I say Godspeed
And if their tempers turn to bitter anger,
Speedy may be their amends.

And so the carriage and pair wait
Outside The Grape's door,
Where at the stroke of midnight
On Saturday 12th October
They will leave for their honeymoon
Loving plastered for their life ahead
Well done Andrea and Carl!
And now the wedding bed!

Gerard Allardyce

I LOVE YOU BECAUSE

I love you because you love beautiful flowers.
I love you because you while away the hours.
I love you because you gaze out at the showers.
I love you because you gaze at me when I'm not looking.
I love you because you still eat my cooking.
I love you because you have to depend on me.
I love you because of the love you give me.
I love you because when I play the fool.
I love you because when in pain as a rule you grin and bear it
                                                    as far as you can.
I love you because you wear my ring.
But most of all, I love you for everything.

Raymond Law

CANDLELIGHT

Candlelight I enjoy your quiet consoling illuminance.
It soothes my troubled thoughts
And lulls the tenseness of my mind
Dispelling the day's depressing clouds of doubt,
Blending my mood to the rhythmic silence of your velvet dance.
Reliant, steadfast, you have always been, shall be,
And like oil, are man's ancient friend.
The genie of darkness before you retreats,
And softly melts away.

Inspiration of incandescent light, yet affinity you share
With lowly glow-worm or brightest star.
I harmonise with your soft glow
As did the muse of long ago.
His thoughts inspired by the cup and your gentle light,
And thus did dream his sweet thoughts of romance and love.
Your sure soft touch will always be there
To enhance a human ceremony.

Steady, sweet as at the altar of repose,
Or at the romance of a table
Where vows of love will outlive the rose
May my troubled thoughts soar away,
Companion with the soot in the tip
Of thy fulfilled flame.
And may my spirit in peace to be the same.

Thomas Wylie

FOOT PLAY

We talked into the night,
the chemistry felt right.
A relationship might
be a delight.

I reached out
and slowly
stroked your shin
with my foot.
(You said it
went straight
to your groin.)

You cradled it in your lap
massaging gently,
caressing my toes,
then bending your head
you sucked them
one by one.
(I didn't tell you
what this did to me.)

Later we kissed,
my body moving against yours
savouring the strength of you,
feeling every muscle to the depths,
shocks of pleasure coursing through me.
We clung to each other.

Chastely we parted,
after all, we'd only just met,
and anticipation
is so delicious.

Valeria Brown

TRUE LOVE

My love's habits in bed
Are not to be discussed by me;
Nor on my habits, I think,
Would she pass comment.

But still I ride the wave
From crest to crest
With the excitement of castles
And many strongholds.

So yet I have to say
Each man should find,
Knowing the world, a lover,
And love her as much as he can.

Tony MacMillan

FIRST LOVE

From the moment I saw you,
I gave you my heart,
I adored you, and thought
That we'd never part.
You were older,
I was too young,
Love was forbidden,
Tho' my feelings so strong!
I never could tell you,
How I loved you
Would have died for you!
To see you passing,
In the street,
My aching heart,
Would miss a beat!
You went away,
To fight the war,
You didn't return
Home any more.
Heartbroken,
I could only cry,
Killed at Tobruk,
In a way, so was I.
I've cherished your memory,
Over the years,
Still-old feelings,
Bring unbidden tears.

E M Eagle

MY DEAR HUSBAND

My dear husband, lover, partner,
You mean everything to me.

Ours is a loving marriage,
A partnership so true.

You are so kind, my loved one,
Nothing is too much trouble.

We work at everything together,
In a loving partnership.

Our only disagreement is -
My inability to pass my driving test.

Janet Cavill

A LOVE SONG

Summer feelings invade, saturate, tingle,
Reality fades, soft warmth, tunes my hidden being.
Each separate feeling tight string, relaxed to a joy.
I dream the sound, all that lives, has the language.
All are born to live, birds of the air, a tree.
A seed, and me all awake, all feel the same melody,
The new air conducts to perfection,
A mighty magic, called joy, demands to be felt.
A love song, played by nature,
The scene is set, all are players.
The Heavens, show invisible, coloured, light
To the little and the large, 'tis so bright.
The wings are bubbling over, to appear.
The magic has happened, with a joy.
That which cannot be altered feels
The song of love.

H Cotterill

WALK INTO THE DARK NIGHT

Walk into the dark night
Where no soul shrieks
Where the de-fleshed heads stare without sight
Mortal life has finished with its lowlands and peaks.

Walk into the dark night
Knowing no one will mourn
The lonely have no support in their last fight
Save their own thoughts at the final dawn.

The dark night draws you away
From the faithless few, who
Gave a guilty shrug, they did not stay
A comfortable life must not be disturbed by you.

Walk into the dark night
But if there is just one who cares
Then at the gate - fight, fight
Turn back to embrace life with one who dares.

J Aldred

LOVE OF ERDINGTON

As I walk around the sun will shine
The spirit of Erdington of charm and love
As grace of beauty remains to be true of history of the grounds
Of heart tears.
Remember how feelings are on our souls love of flowers on
Grave sides to make peace with Lord above us.
Not how people say words on churches to pray.
If I had one thing to say I was brought up in Erdington and proud
Of it.
I became a poet in 1995 until end of the century I reign my poems
All the great books.
As Jo the Poet I am called as they know everywhere in
Erdington.

Josephine Teresa Elliott

WATER WHEEL

You flow through me like water
rushing, dragged by
the unstoppable lunar pull
of seas and tides.
Waves of confusion
crash into agonising clarity.

Everything is circular
a sphere.
And here
is a water wheel
pouring right through you
washing, sucking in,
drowning in murky
mouthfuls of it as
that salt water wave leaves me
senseless, hopeless again.
Until I realise
there is no rain
under the surface.

R H Galloway

FOR ANDY

You are everything
And more
My heart is tied to yours
Please be careful
A slight inflection of voice
Might crush me completely
Or release me to fly
For you, you are my everything
You are everything
And more.

Emma Ayling

TO SOMEONE WHO CARED
(Dedicated to Margaret and for Davey)

To someone who loved me unconditionally
To someone who cared.
To someone who always believed in me while others didn't.
To someone who when I needed a home, a friend or someone to talk to,
                        you were there.
To someone who, when after James Jnr died, you knew my sense
                           of loss and pain.
And while everyone else had forgotten him, you didn't,
You understood and knew how much we loved him.
To someone who made my life worth living.
To someone I give you my sincere thanks, and I will always remember
                   and love you for everything you did for me.
And this is to someone who cared.

Bernadette C Curran